Dedicated to YOU!

Contents

The Little Children's
BIBLE
STORYBOOK

Retold by Anne de Graaf
Illustrated by José Pérez Montero

SCANDINAVIA

The Little Children's Bible Storybook

2nd edition, 1st print
Copyright © Scandinavia Publishing House, 2016
Drejervej 15, 3., DK-2400 Copenhagen NV, Denmark
www.sph.as info@sph.as
Text copyright © 2011 Anne de Graaf
Illustration copyright © 2011 José Pérez Montero
Edited by Cecilie Fodor
Design by Gao Hanyu

Printed in China
ISBN 9788772030142

The Old Testament

God Makes
the World

Genesis 1-3

Close your eyes.
Hold your breath. *Shhhh.*

There was nothing in the
beginning... except for God.

Turn the light off.
Turn the light on.

God took the darkness and
changed it, so that suddenly...
there was light.

God made the earth. He made the sun and moon, all the planets, and the stars.

How many stars? One? Two? Three? Four? God made more, and more, and more, and more, and more. . .

God made the oceans and the seas. He made fish, and more, and more, and more fish.

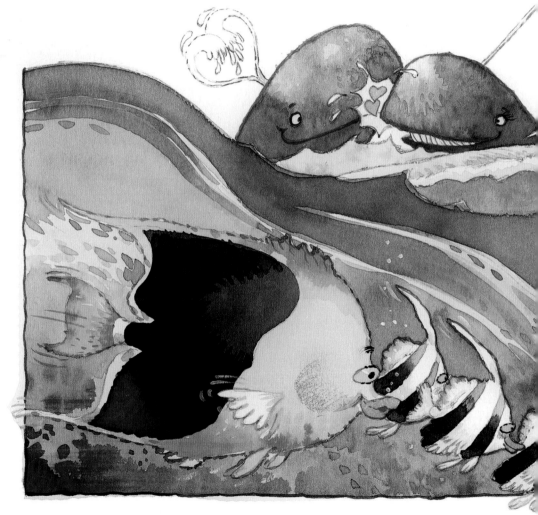

God made the land. He made
animals, and more, and more, and
more animals.

19

When God had had finished making , He then
made the first man and called him Adam.
God made a helper and friend for Adam and
named her Eve.

Just like He made you-- your fingers,
your toes, your smile, too.

Adam and Eve lived
in a special garden
called Eden. God had one
rule: Do not eat the fruit
from one tree.
God said, "No."
The serpent told Eve, "Yes."

Eve chose to break the rule, and
then so did Adam. This was wrong.

What rules do you know?

When Adam and Eve did not listen, they had to leave Eden. They never, ever felt as close to God again.

But God went on loving Adam and Eve, though. No matter what, He always loves. God gave two sons to Adam and Eve. Every child is a gift from God.

That means YOU are a big wiggly present! To whom?

Noah
and the Ark

Genesis 6-8

A long, long, long,
long time ago,
no one said, "Thank You!"
to God anymore.

Everyone chose to be bad. This made God very sad. One man was different. His name was Noah.

He talked to God and listened to God.

Name all the things and people you can say, "Thank You!" to God for.

God told Noah, "There will be a huge flood. Build a boat. Build a BIG boat. Build a VERY BIG boat!"
Noah's boat was called an ark.
Noah's neighbors laughed at Noah. "We live in the desert!
Where's the water?"

Whom did Noah listen to?
Whom do you hear now?

God said to fill the boat, the B*I*G
boat, the VERY B*I*G boat with two
of every animal. God promised
to keep Noah, his family, and the
animals safe, inside the ark.

Then, it started to rain and rain. It rained for forty days and forty nights. All those animals! All those days and nights! All that rain!

Noah's ark floated higher and higher, higher even than the mountaintops. As water covered the earth, all the living things of the earth drowned.

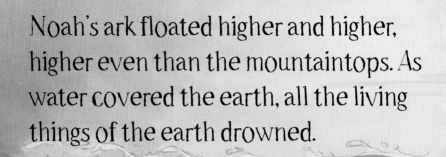

Finally, the rain stopped.
Then God sent a wind.

Make a sound like the rain.
Now, make a sound like the
wind.

Noah and God's Promise

Genesis 8

Water was every-where! Noah sent a raven to look for dry land.

Noah and the animals in the ark waited and waited for the water to go down. After the raven, Noah sent out a dove. TWICE!

Can you make flapping sounds like a bird? TWICE!

The second time, the dove returned with an olive leaf in its beak. This meant that somewhere there were places dry enough for trees and plants to grow.

God said to Noah, "You, your family, and all the animals may leave the boat. Go onto the land and build homes."

God kept his promise. He kept
Noah and his family and all the
animals safe and sound.

Show how the kangaroos
got off the ark. And the
snakes? Do you think
there's more to this story?

Noah and God's Gift

Genesis 8–9

Noah thanked God for keeping them safe.
Then God gave Noah a gift.

God's gift to Noah, and to us, is the rainbow. This is God's sign that he always keeps his promises.

Just as the colors are endless, so the rainbow is endless. And just like the rainbow, God's love goes on, and on, and on. . .

The Beginning of the Tower of Babel

Genesis 11

Where do you live? What country? Do
you know how to say "Hi!" in any other
languages?

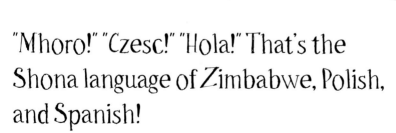

"Mhoro!" "Czesc!" "Hola!" That's the Shona language of Zimbabwe, Polish, and Spanish!

A long, long, long time ago,
everyone spoke only one language.

We speak the same language.
Say "Hi!" Say it louder! I hear
you and say "Hi!" back.

Then, some people found a flat place and
decided to make it their home.

I like flat places. They are easy to build on. The next time you play in the sand, clear a flat place before you build your tower.

The people said, "Let's make bricks and bake them until they're very hard."

What happens when you kick a tower made of sand? *Whooosh!* What happens when you kick one made of bricks? *Ouch!!!!*

The people were
clever. Instead of
using stones, they
made bricks, and
stuck the bricks
together with tar,
instead of mortar.

Build a tower with your fists, one on top of the other, on top of the other, on top of the other... Where will it stop?

The End of the Tower of Babel

Genesis 11

Oh, yes! They were building the Tower of Babel up to the sky!

These people said, "We can be famous and not have to wander anymore."

Then, the people said, "Come, let's build ourselves a city! We will finally have a home."

Now just a tower wasn't good enough. They had great plans!

When God saw what the people were trying to do, He knew He must stop them, or they would think they were gods.

They grew way too proud of themselves and their plans for a great tower and a great city.

So, God mixed up their words and made different languages. The people no longer spoke one language, but many.

If workers don't understand each other, One could say, "Get that grain of sand!" and another might think he meant, "Hand me the hammer!" That's no way to build something.

The city they never finished building was called Babel, which means "mixed up and confused" because there the Lord mixed up the language of the whole world.

No matter how high you reach, or how big you dream, thank and praise God for helping you. Always include God in your plans.

Then, the
Lord sent all
the people
wandering,
spreading them
out all over
the earth.

"Goodbye!"
"Adiós!"
"Czesc!"
"Chisaraizvakanaka!"

Abraham
Follows God

Genesis 12-13, 17

Abraham had many sheep, cattle and
camels. He and Sarah lived in the desert
and slept in tents.

One night, God told Abraham He would make his family into a great nation. Abraham believed God and trusted Him.

What nation are you a part of? Would you believe God if He told you something amazing?

God also promised Abraham and Sarah a new homeland. So they packed their tents onto camels and traveled until God told them when and where to stop.

Pack your bags! Who's the leader here?

Abraham's Great Big Family

Genesis 13, 15, 17-18, 21

Many years went by and Abraham and Sarah STILL didn't have a child. They asked God, "Why?" How many stars are there? A million? A billion? Can you count them? This is how great and large a family God promised Abraham and Sarah.

One day, three strangers visited Abraham and Sarah, who served them their best food. One of the visitors said Sarah would soon have a son.

More than anything else, Abraham and Sarah wanted a baby, a child just like you!

Sarah was listening from inside the tent. She laughed because she was now very old, too old to have a baby.

The visitor said, "Why did Sarah laugh? Nothing is too hard for the Lord to do."

94

Sarah was baffled by what she heard, but Abraham knew that the visitor was the Lord.

A year later, Abraham and Sarah finally had their little boy, Isaac, God's own gift. Isaac was the beginning of the great, big family God promised Abraham.
Isaac means Laughter.

Whom did Isaac make happy when he was born?
Whom did you make happy when you were born?

Joseph and the Colorful Coat

Genesis 37

Isaac had a son named Jacob. Jacob grew up and had twelve sons. Joseph was his favorite. One day, Jacob gave him a colorful coat. This made the other brothers jealous.

Have you ever had a dream? What did you dream about?

One night, Joseph dreamed the sun, moon and eleven stars bowed down to him, as if he were a king. His older brothers did not like this. "We'll never bow down to YOU!"

Joseph went to check on his brothers who were watching over the sheep. His brothers took his special coat and threw him in a well.

Joseph's brothers sold him as a slave to Egypt-- far, far away. But God was with Joseph.

Joseph
Forgives His Brothers

Genesis 39–46

Joseph worked very hard as a slave in Egypt. The man who owned Joseph put him in charge of his home and farm. Joseph worked for God and thought of Him as his REAL Master. What did you work hard at today?

In Egypt, God helped Joseph see what dreams meant. Pharaoh, the king of Egypt, told Joseph about a dream where seven fat cows crossed the river.

110

God showed Joseph that the fat cows meant seven good years.
So, Pharaoh freed Joseph and put him in charge of storing food.

After the seven good years came
seven bad years. That's what the
skinny cows stood for! Then, because
it was so hard to find food, Joseph's
brothers came to Egypt. They did
not recognize Joseph, but Joseph
recognized them.

When Joseph looked into their eyes, he could not be mad at his brothers. What color are the eyes of the person reading you this story?

Joseph forgave
his brothers for
the mean trick they
had played on him
so long ago. God
had taken care of
Joseph, that was all
that mattered. The
brothers jumped for
joy at finding each
other again!

Have you ever been mad at someone? Did you forgive them?

Jacob and his sons moved to Egypt to be near Joseph. Now their family was together again!

Moses Hears the Call of God

Exodus 1-4

The king of Egypt, or Pharaoh, wanted to hurt Hebrew babies like Moses. So, his mother put him in a basket and sent him floating down a river.

God kept Moses safe. Pharaoh's daughter heard Moses crying. She saved him and made Moses her own son.

Moses grew up in the palace. The Egyptians hated the Hebrews, who were God's people. One day, Moses saw an Egyptian hitting a Hebrew man. Moses killed the Egyptian and ran away.

Moses married a woman from Midian. One day, when he was tending his father-in-law's sheep, Moses saw a bush on fire, but the fire was not really burning the bush! How could that be?

It was God, trying to get Moses to listen!

What was God calling Moses to do? To go back to Egypt and help save God's people from the Egyptians. But Moses was afraid and said, "Not me, God."

What was Moses afraid of?

God knew Moses could not
talk well, but God said he
would fix that.
All Moses had to do was
listen to God's call and
just say, "Yes."

How easy is it to just say "Yes"? Do you
ever find it hard to obey?

Moses Leads God's People

Exodus 5–34;
Numbers 13–14;
Deuteronomy 1

Moses led the people out of Egypt. Then God split the Red Sea right in half!

Moses obeyed God and returned to Egypt. He asked Pharaoh to release God's people. But Pharaoh's heart was hardened, and he said, "No!" God showed His power in many ways until finally Pharaoh gave in. Later, Pharaoh changed his mind. He cried out to his soldiers, "Go after them and bring them back!" But God was watching over His people. Just as Moses' group reached the Red Sea, God made the waters split open! They all reached the other side safely before God closed the waters again.

During the long journey to the Promised Land, God's people started to forget to worship and praise God.

So God wrote in stone ten rules for Moses and His people to follow.

God gave these rules to keep His children safe, healthy, and happy.

Have you ever heard your stomach grumbling? That's what God's people did in the desert — they grumbled!

When God's people arrived at the promised land, called Canaan. they still grumbled against God. He made them wander in the desert for forty years until they learned to trust Him. Despite their grumbling, God gave his people food and water every day.

Ruth Must Find a New Home

Ruth 1-2

There once was a young woman named Ruth, who married a man from another country.

It looks like she loves him very much!

One day, Ruth's husband died.
His mother, Naomi, told Ruth, "You should
go back home to your own parents."
Naomi wanted to return to her home,
and God's people in Israel.

In which country were you born? Is that the same country you live in now?

Ruth was very special because she loved God, And she loved Naomi, who had taught her to love God.

141

Ruth begged Naomi, "Please let me go with you. I will go where you go. Your people will be my people and your God, my God. He will take care of us."

Point to things that are the same color as the colors of your country's flag.

In what city were you born?
Is that your home now?

Naomi and Ruth walked a long, long way.
They walked all the way to Bethlehem,
the city where Naomi was born, their
new home!

God Rewards Ruth's Loyalty

Ruth 2-4

In Bethlehem, Ruth took care of Naomi. She gathered leftover grain and shared it with Naomi.

The field where Ruth found food belonged
to a man named Boaz.
Boaz wanted to help Ruth because she was
helping Naomi.

Boaz let Ruth take home as much grain as she wanted. Naomi said, "Does Boaz own the field? He is a relative of mine!"

Naomi told Ruth, "Because Boaz is from my family and cares about us, maybe he will marry you."

Ruth and Boaz were married and there was a big party. Naomi was very, very happy!

Who loves you? Does that make you happy? Show how happy you are by smiling the biggest smile in the world!

Now, Ruth and Boaz could take care of Naomi together. After a while, they had a little baby boy called Obed. Naomi was like a grandmother to Obed.

Does someone who loves you have a special name for you? Do you have a special name you call them?

Many, many years later, King David was born in Bethlehem. Many, many years after that, Jesus was born in Bethlehem. They were both part of the same family, with Obed as a great-great-great grandfather, and Ruth, Obed's mother.

God Chooses David

1 Samuel 16

God looked at the heart of a shepherd
boy named David, and saw David loved
Him very much.

159

David liked to play his harp
and sing songs for God.

Can you look at your heart?
Can you feel it? Do you feel good when you do good?

David was also very good at slinging
stones. He could hit whatever he aimed
at. He could even kill bears that hunted
his sheep!

He could EVEN kill lions with his sling!

A wise man named Samuel came to David's family to find God's choice for king. Not this brother, not this one, not this one, not this one, not this one, not this one, not this one!

"Are these seven boys all of your sons?" Samuel asked. "No," David's father answered, "I have one more, the youngest." Samuel chose David because God had plans for David. Not then, but someday David would become king.

Sometimes being the youngest isn't so bad.

David Fights Goliath

1 Samuel 17

The army of *Israel* was mighty and great in number. Still, the soldiers were very, VERY scared of fighting the giant GOLIATH!

What is a bully?

173

No one in the army dared to fight Goliath.
David was too small to be in the army, like
his brothers, but he still begged King Saul,
"Let me fight Goliath! I'm good with a sling."

David knew God was on his side.

The giant, named Goliath, was making fun of God and God's people. "You're nothing, and so is your God!" This was a terrible thing to say.

David said, "Oh, yeah? You're not too big for my God!"

Has anyone ever made fun of you because you're the smallest or youngest?

David took aim at the giant and sent a stone whistling through the air with his sling. The stone flew and flew until… *PING!* It hit Goliath in the head and killed him!

It's not always the big and strong who win. Sometimes it's the small and brave.

179

After David killed Goliath, everyone said, "Three cheers for young David! Hip, hip hooray! Young David is brave and handsome."

Was David special because he was smart and brave and handsome and good? No. He was special because God chose him and loved him. Just like you are special because God loves YOU!

Jonah Tries to Run from God

Jonah 1

There once was a man named Jonah. God told Jonah to go to Nineveh and said, "Go warn your enemies to change their ways."

"Warn my enemies?" Jonah said. "I don't want to warn my enemies, the Ninevites. I want God to punish them." So Jonah chose not to go to Nineveh. Instead he decided to go to Tarshish in Spain.

I've often wanted to go to Spain. How about you?

Instead of heading toward Nineveh, Jonah went to Joppa, got on a ship, and sailed for Spain. He thought he could run away from God.

To get somewhere, you can go straight, or you can walk sideways like me. Try it!

But Jonah couldn't run away from God. God is everywhere. Jonah disobeyed, so God sent a terrible storm.

Show how the boat went back and forth, up and down. Now show how the boat went WAY UP AND WAY DOWN!!

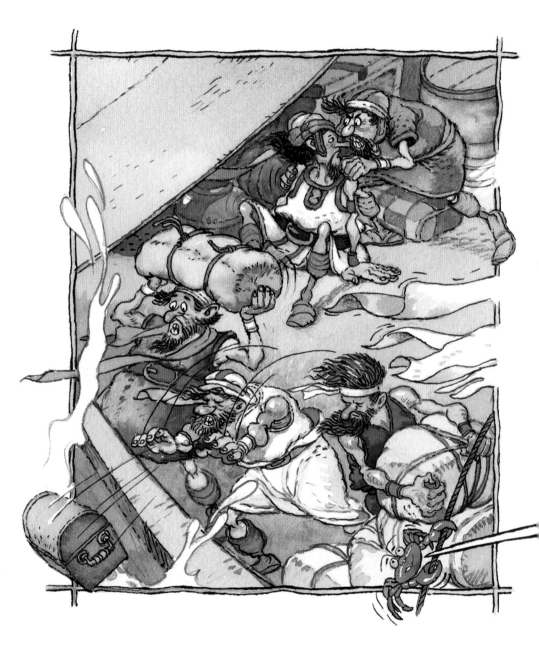

The sailors didn't know what to do! First they threw all the cargo overboard. Then, they woke up Jonah. "What did you do to make God send this storm?"

The sailors wanted to know how to stop the storm. The wind was blowing very fast! Try blowing as hard as the wind!

Jonah said, "This storm is all my fault. Throw me overboard and you'll be safe." The sailors didn't want to, but they had no choice.

They picked up Jonah and *one, two, three, heave ho!* Into the raging sea he went with a great big SPLASH! Can you make bubble sounds (even though you're NOT underwater?)

Down, down, down, into the sea Jonah went. The storm stopped, but Jonah didn't notice since he kept sinking deeper, and deeper, and deeper.

Jonah and the Big Fish

Jonah 1-4

GULP! For three days and nights Jonah stayed in the big fish's belly. Finally, Jonah prayed and said he was sorry. Then, God had the fish spit him out on a beach.

God still wanted Jonah to go to Nineveh--
not Spain, or anywhere else. Nineveh. So
this time, what **did** Jonah do? *FINALLY*, he
went to Nineveh.

Jonah spent one whole day wandering
up and down the streets. He told his
enemies to stop doing evil things or
God would punish them.

201

Guess what? The Ninevites listened! "Oh! We're so sorry!" they cried. They put on clothes that looked like sacks to show God how sorry they were.

Even the king was sorry. He took off his rich robes and put on sackcloth like the rest of the Ninevites.

God forgave the Ninevites. They heard His message and obeyed.

Everyone prayed and asked God to save them.

And that's what God wanted.

When God chose to forgive the Ninevites, Jonah was not happy. He was mad and went off by himself. God caused a plant to grow and shade Jonah.

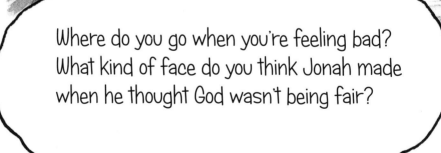

Where do you go when you're feeling bad? What kind of face do you think Jonah made when he thought God wasn't being fair?

207

Then God had a worm attack the plant and make it die. Now Jonah was REALLY mad. But God told Jonah, "You cared about the plant. Think of how much more I care about all those men and women and children. They are why I sent you to Nineveh!"

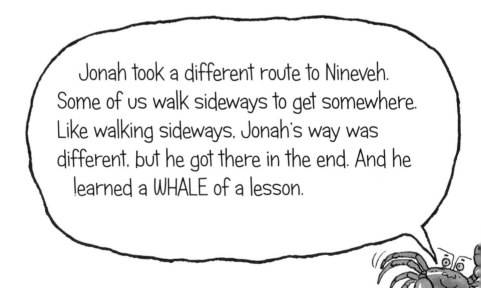

Jonah took a different route to Nineveh. Some of us walk sideways to get somewhere. Like walking sideways, Jonah's way was different, but he got there in the end. And he learned a WHALE of a lesson.

Esther
the Beautiful

Esther 1

The king had the most beautiful women brought to the palace. There, they waited a year to hear who would be chosen as queen. They ate the best food, wore the prettiest makeup and sweetest perfumes, and were given the best massages.

Rub the shoulders of the person reading to you. Now it's your turn!

One of the girls was named Esther. She was very special, and not just because she was so beautiful. Esther was special because she was keeping a special secret. Esther's secret was that she was a Jew, one of God's chosen people.

What was your most fun, all-time favorite secret? Come on, you can tell me!

When it was Esther's turn to meet the king, there was no contest! He chose her and she became Queen Esther.

What do you think was so beautiful about Esther? What do you think God saw in Esther that was beautiful?

218

Queen Esther Saves Her People

Esther 2-7

A man named Haman ordered the deaths of all the Jewish people throughout the land! So all the Jews prayed to God, asking for help. Do you pray to God when you need help?

The king loved Esther, but did not know she was Jewish. When a new and terrible law ordered all Jews to be killed, Esther prayed to God, then went to the king.

Esther knew the king could have her killed for coming to see him without being invited. Would he be angry?

The king smiled when he saw Esther. "Of course I will see you, Esther. What do you wish from me?" Esther trusted God. She asked the king to dinner, and there, she told the king everything!

If you were the king or queen, what would you order for dinner every day?

The king helped Esther. Afterward, they celebrated by giving gifts to the poor. Then, the Jews threw a huge party and called it the Feast of Purim, in honor of when God used Esther the brave and beautiful to save the Jewish people.

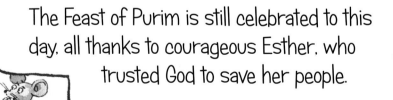

The Feast of Purim is still celebrated to this day, all thanks to courageous Esther, who trusted God to save her people.

225

The New Testament

Mary
and Joseph

Matthew 1; Luke 1

The Christmas story began with a girl named Mary being woken up by a bright light. An angel told her, "Mary, you are very special. God has chosen you to become the mother of Jesus, God's Son."

God also sent an angel to Joseph in a
dream. The angel said, "Don't be afraid
to make Mary your wife. She is telling
the truth about the baby. He is God's
Son. You will call him Jesus."

And that's who Christmas is about.
Baby Jesus.

When Jesus was almost ready to be born, Mary and Joseph had to make a long trip. They had to travel all the way from Nazareth to Bethlehem.

Jesus was growing in Mary's tummy. Do you know anyone who is going to have a baby? You can pray for that baby now.

When Mary and Joseph arrived in Bethlehem, there was no place for them to stay! The city was full of people. Everywhere they tried, they heard the same thing.

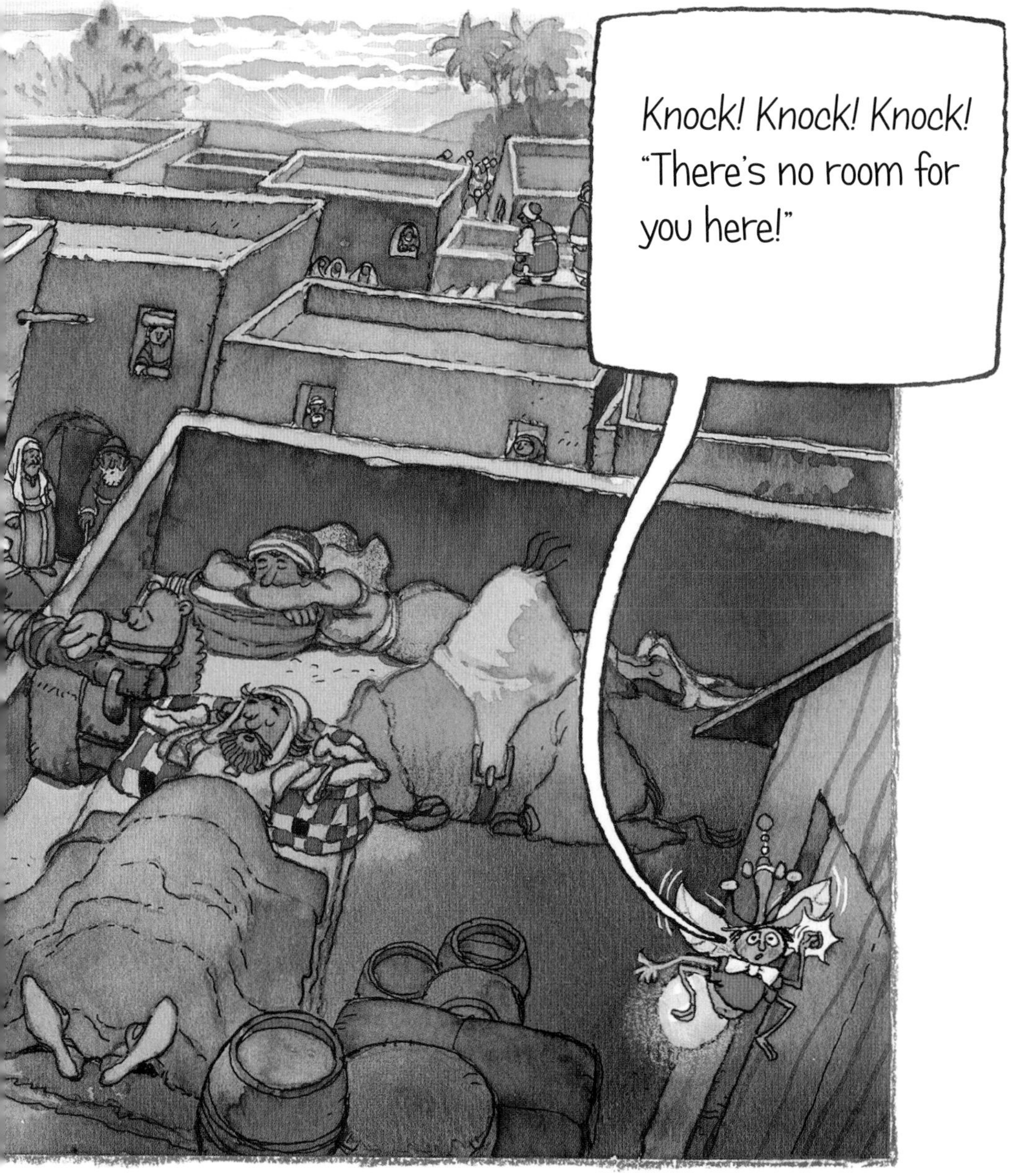
Knock! Knock! Knock!
"There's no room for you here!"

The First Christmas

Matthew 1-2; Luke 2

On the night Jesus was born, shepherds in
the nearby hills saw angels singing in the sky.
"Glory to God! A Savior is born!"

The shepherds said, "Look!"

That night the shepherds ran to
a cave in the hillside. "Look!"

Inside, they found a stable, two new parents and the tiny, newborn Baby Jesus.

Mary and Joseph took Baby Jesus to the temple. An old man, named Simeon, blessed Jesus. He said, "Now I have seen the Light who will save all people." An old woman named Anna said, "Yes. He is the Savior."

What are the two other names Jesus is called here?

Three wise men who lived far away from Bethlehem saw a giant star. They rode their camels a long way to find out what the bright star meant. They called Baby Jesus the King of the Jews.

Lie down under a Christmas tree and squint your eyes. Maybe then the lights will look like stars.

These three wise men brought Jesus
fantastic gifts fit for a king.

They gave Jesus gold, a rich perfume
called myrrh, and frankincense, which
smells sweet when burned.

Jesus is the Light who helps us see, the Light who shows us the Way. THAT'S what Christmas is about-- Baby Jesus.

Jesus is called Light of the World. On this first Christmas, Jesus was God's present to us.

Simon Peter the Rock

Matthew 4, 5–10, 12, 14–16, 19–20;
Mark 1, 3, 6, 8, 10;
Luke 4–9, 11, 18;
John 1, 3–4, 6, 9;
Acts 8–12, 15;
Galatians 2;
1 and 2 Peter

There once was a fisherman named Simon. One day, Simon was fishing with his brother. Jesus called them saying, "Come, follow me." Jesus chose Simon plus eleven other men to be his closest followers, or disciples.

Simon and the other disciples
followed Jesus from village to
village, listening and learning.

The crowds grew larger every time
Jesus taught. "Follow me," he called
to the people.

Play follow-the-leader. March around the room, then turn around. Now who's following?

Simon watched Jesus help the blind people to see and the lame to walk. Simon could not believe his eyes.

Simon followed Jesus for over two years. The more he listened to Jesus and knew His heart, the more he loved Him. One day, Jesus told him, "Your name is Simon, but from now on you will be called Peter."

Jesus said, "Someday you will lead the people who follow me. They are my church. You will become the rock, or foundation, on which the church is built." Peter means Rock.

Peter followed Jesus, and spent the rest of his life helping others to follow Jesus. Later in life, he bravely led the Christians. Peter became a true fisher of men.

The Miracles of Jesus

Matthew 9; Mark 2; Luke 5, 17; John 2, 11

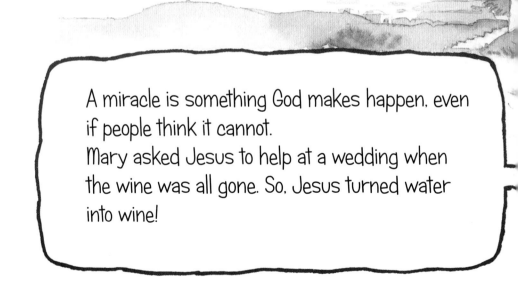

A miracle is something God makes happen, even if people think it cannot.

Mary asked Jesus to help at a wedding when the wine was all gone. So, Jesus turned water into wine!

Once, when Jesus was inside a house teaching, somebody cut a hole in the ceiling! Four men lowered down a man who could not walk., and Jesus healed him.

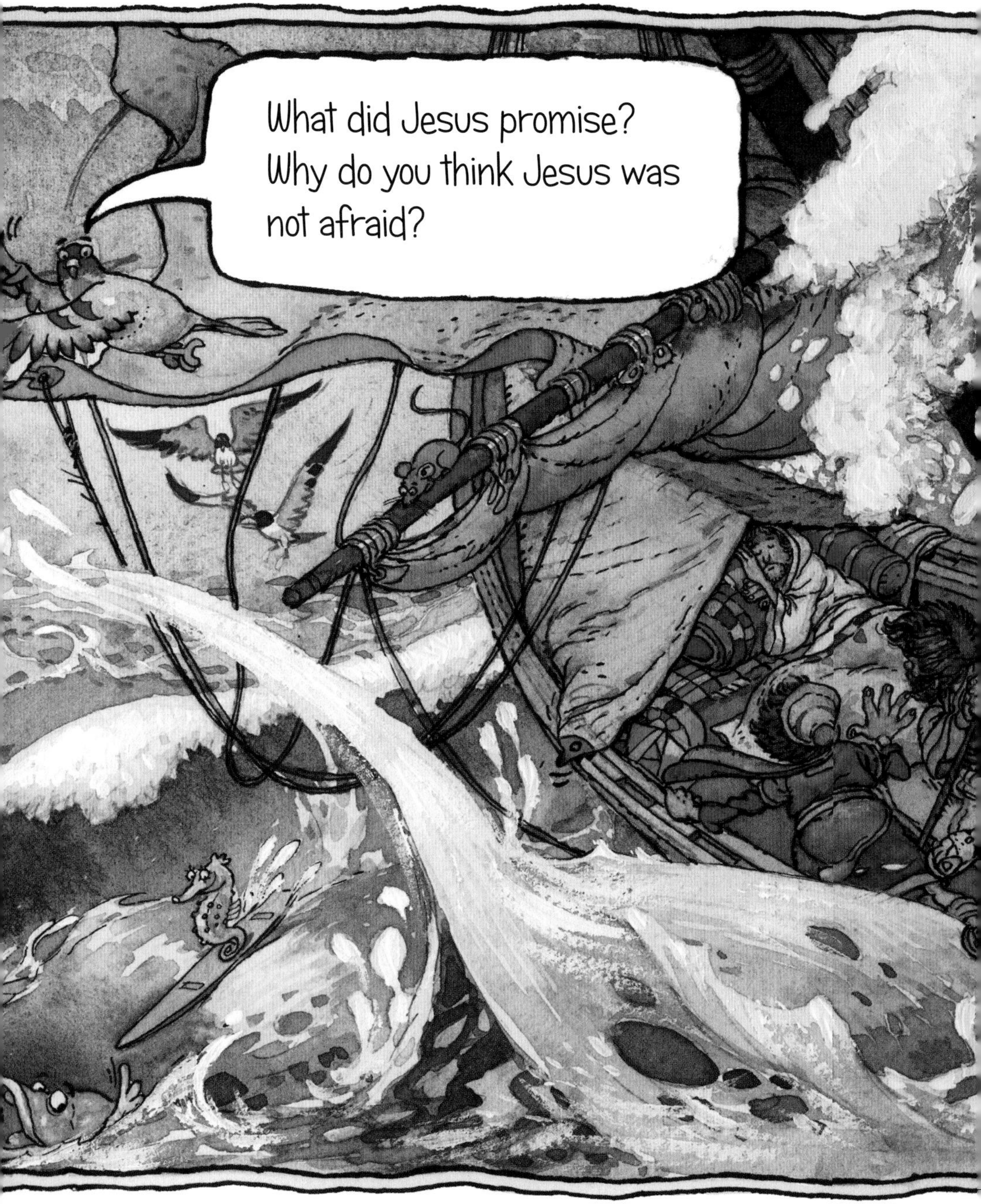
What did Jesus promise? Why do you think Jesus was not afraid?

One day, Jesus and his disciples were out
sailing, when a great storm suddenly began.
Huge waves crashed over the boat and the
disciples were afraid they would all drown,
but Jesus was fast asleep on a cushion.

Stand up and spread your arms. That's how Jesus stood in the boat. Next time you feel unsure, remember God's words and promises to us.

Jesus had said they would go to the other side of the lake. The disciples should have trusted Jesus words.

There once were ten very sick men. "Please help us!" they begged Jesus. So Jesus healed them, too. Only one man came back to say "Thank you," to Jesus.

One day, a sick woman reached through the crowd and touched Jesus' robe. He felt her touch and said, "Your faith has made you whole." She was healed!

Mary, Martha, and their brother Lazarus were all good friends of Jesus. While Jesus was away, Lazarus became very sick and died. Jesus came back and made Lazarus live again!

What is a miracle? YOU are a miracle! Jesus made you and that is the most special miracle of all!

The Stories of Jesus

Matthew 7; Luke 6, 11–12, 15; John 10

Jesus taught about God's love by telling stories. These are just a few of Jesus' favorites.

Jesus said not to worry about food and clothes. God knows what people need. Jesus told his followers that they were more valuable than the flowers that grow and the birds that fly. Yet God takes good care of the flowers and birds, too.

Jesus told another story about a man who kept knocking and knocking on his neighbor's door because he needed to borrow some bread for another friend. He kept knocking until the man finally opened the door and gave him some bread.

What happens when you knock on a door? Try it now. When you pray, it is like knocking on the door to heaven. God always hears your prayers, no matter how softly you whisper them. You can talk to Him in prayer anytime you want to.

In another story, Jesus said we should build our lives on Him like a house built on solid rock, not sand.

What happens to a sand castle at the beach when the wind and waves come? *WHOOSH!* All gone!

Jesus taught that a good
shepherd does all he can to
save his sheep. He does not
run away when a wolf comes.

Jesus told the story of a young man who wanted more. He wanted more money, more things, more friends, and he wanted to travel more, so he left home. This was a sad day for his father.

Soon, the young man ran out of money, so he took a job feeding pigs. The pigs were getting more food than he was, so he went back home. There, his father welcomed him with open arms.

Nothing is more important than the love of God. Can you go hug someone you love?

Jesus and the Children

Matthew 14, 19; Mark 6, 10;
Luke 9, 18; John 6

Jesus' friends once told some children, "Go away. Leave Jesus alone!" Jesus told them, "No! Let the children come to me."

Jesus liked to teach children of all ages. Once, at the end of a long day, Jesus' friends said, "Send everyone home. They're all so hungry." But Jesus said there was more He wanted to teach.

A little boy stepped forward.
"*I* have some fish and bread, Sir.
I will share, but it's not much."

All the people grew still.
Jesus looked up. He called
out to God and thanked
His Father for the food.
Then, Jesus blessed the
bread and broke it into
many pieces.

Surprise! There was more bread and more fish, more than enough for everyone! With Jesus' blessing, one little child like you can make a BIG difference.

Jesus in Jerusalem

Matthew 21, 26–27; Mark 11, 14–15;
Luke 19, 22–23; John 12–13, 18

When Jesus entered Jerusalem, the people cheered for him in a parade. They waved palm branches up and down. Wave your hands. *Hooray* for Jesus!

The temple leaders did not like Jesus.
They paid his apostle, Judas, thirty pieces
of silver to help them trap Jesus.

Why do you think these people didn't like Jesus?

In Jerusalem, Jesus thanked God for the bread and wine. He broke the bread into pieces, and passed the bread and wine to his friends.

Judas led Jesus' enemies right to Him. Peter fought back! He cut off the ear of a guard. Jesus taught people to love their enemies. He picked up the ear and healed the guard.

Jesus taught that we should not hurt people —even when we are angry.

Jesus' enemies brought him before a judge.
"Kill him on the cross!" they screamed. What
terrible words Jesus' enemies said! Did Jesus
do anything wrong? Did he get angry at his
enemies? No!

The First Easter

Matthew 27-28; Mark 15-16; Luke 23-24; John 14, 19-21; Acts 1

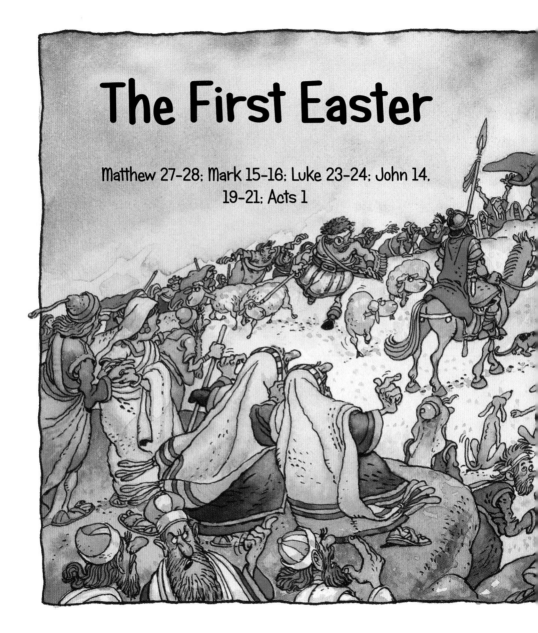

Jesus' enemies nailed Him to a cross, where He died. His friends and family were crying and very sad. They took Him down off the cross, and placed Him gently in a special cave. Guards were standing outside.

This story is about new life through Jesus. When Jesus died, everything seemed very dark —just like it will be inside my cocoon.

A few days later, Jesus' friends came back to the cave. It was empty! "Where is Jesus?" they cried. The guards didn't know anything.

See if you can find signs of the miracle of new life outside-- a tiny tree, a flower, the morning sun.

An angel said, "Fear not. Are you looking for Jesus? Jesus is alive again! He's not dead! Be happy! Go in and look where he used to lay. Now, go tell everyone that he's alive." The women ran off, hardly believing their eyes and ears.

Look at what happened to me! Do you think it was a miracle? On which holiday do we remember this story?

After Jesus rose from the dead, He visited His friends who were fishing and said, "Throw your net out again!" Then, they caught so many fish, the net almost burst!

Which season is Easter in? Not winter, autumn, or summer! SPRING! Spring is the time for baby lambs and butterflies. It is a time for new life. We have new life when we believe in Jesus and follow Him.

Jesus spent forty days visiting and teaching His friends. Once, He said, "In heaven there are many rooms. I will get them ready for you." Then Jesus went to heaven.

Paul's Change of Heart

Acts 7-9, 11, 13-28; Epistles of Paul

Saul was someone
who hurt Jesus' friends.

323

Saul hurt Jesus' friends until one day when a bright light blinded him.

Saul heard Jesus' voice say, "When you hurt My followers, you hurt Me." Then, God helped Saul see that Jesus is the Son of God.

When Jesus helped Saul to see again,
He gave Saul a new name. From then on he
was called Paul. After his change of heart,
Paul traveled far and wide, telling everyone
he met about Jesus' love.

Greece and Turkey are two of the countries Paul visited. Can you find them on a map?

Jesus' enemies threw Paul and his friend and helper, Silas, into prison. But, inside the prison, Paul and Silas could still pray and sing songs about God's love.

Can you sing a song for Jesus?

The more Paul talked to people about Jesus, the more often Jesus' enemies arrested and hurt Paul.

During his many years in jail, Paul wrote several letters to his friends. He taught of Jesus and God's love.

Does your family write letters?

Jesus' enemies arrested Paul. Because of this, he had to go to Rome, Italy. To get there, he had to travel by boat.

Then a storm came. The storm raged and blew day after day, night after night. Some of the men wanted to jump off the ship, but Paul said, "Unless these men stay on the ship, they cannot be saved!"

Cup your hands around your mouth. Can you howl like the wind in a storm?

Paul started his journey as an enemy of Jesus. But Paul had a change of heart. He ended up traveling far and wide, spreading the Good News that Jesus lives and forgives!

A journey is a trip. On every trip, short or long, be sure to remember the Good News that Jesus loves you.

God Promises a New World

Revelation 1, 19-22

John was a follower of Jesus.

When John was an old man, he had a vision, which was a special message from God. He wrote down Jesus' words, "I'm here for anyone who asks Me into their lives. I'm standing at the door, knocking, waiting for them to hear My voice and open the door."

Go to the door, close it, then have the person reading to you knock on it. Opening the door and letting them in is like asking Jesus into your own heart.

In John's vision, he heard music and saw a huge crowd, the followers of Jesus from all time and all countries. No one could count all the people!

343

John's vision of heaven shows us what God's kingdom will be like. There will be no more bad people, and no more sadness.

Name three things that you think will be in Heaven.

In John's vision he saw that those who had chosen to follow Jesus were there with God. He said heaven was a place of light and happiness.

John wrote often about light, living in the light, and God's kingdom as a place of light. Turn the light on and off now. Who is the Light of the World?

John wrote
that Jesus said, "Listen!
I am coming soon. I was in the
beginning of all things, and I
will be there at the end."

In the beginning there was darkness. In the
end with Jesus there is light. Pray now with
the person reading to you, the last words
John wrote:

"Come, Lord Jesus!"